RIDEAU HALL

CANADA'S LIVING HERITAGE

PREFACE
Their Excellencies
The Right Honourable
Ramon John Hnatyshyn
and Mrs. Gerda Hnatyshyn

PUBLISHED BY
Friends of Rideau Hall

ii

Publisher
  Friends of Rideau Hall

Co-authors
  Gerda Hnatyshyn
  Paulette Lachapelle-Bélisle

Photography
  Gene Hattori

Graphic Designer
  Colin Davis

Contributing Writers
  Lesley Lynn
  E. Russell Smith

Artistic Direction
  Paulette Lachapelle-Bélisle

Project Support
  Annick Brie
  Nancy Davies

Financial Advisor
  JoAnn MacKenzie

Electronic Imaging
  TrueColor Graphics Ltd.,
  Saskatoon, Saskatchewan.

Photographic Equipment
  Andy Petersons,
  Lisle Kelco Ltd.
  Toronto, Ontario.

Paper Merchants
  Coast Paper,
  Saskatoon, Saskatchewan.

Paper supplied
  Island Paper Mills,
  New Westminster,
  British Columbia.

Printed and bound in Canada by
  D.W. Friesen and Sons Ltd.,
  Winnipeg, Manitoba.

Distributor
  Friends of Rideau Hall
  P.O. Box 7158
  Vanier Station
  Vanier, Ontario
  K1L 5A0

All proceeds will be used to continue the historical restoration of Rideau Hall.

Inquiries regarding contributions to the Collection should be addressed to:
  Friends of Rideau Hall
  P.O. Box 7158, Vanier Station
  Vanier, Ontario K1L 5A0

Copyright © 1994
Friends of Rideau Hall

CANADIAN CATALOGUING
IN PUBLICATION DATA

Hnatyshyn, Gerda. Date
Rideau Hall: Canada's living heritage

Includes
bibliographical references.
ISBN 0-9699028-0-8

1. Rideau Hall (Ottawa, Ont.).
2. Ottawa (Ont.) – Buildings, structures, etc.
3. McKay, Thomas, 1792-1855.
4. Governors General. – Homes and haunts – Ontario – Ottawa.
I. Lachapelle-Bélisle, Paulette. Date II. Friends of Rideau Hall.
III. Title.

FC3096.8.R5H58 1994
971.3'84 C94-900921-0
F1059.5.09H58 1994

iv

ACKNOWLEDGEMENTS

Rideau Hall: Canada's Living Heritage is dedicated to the many generous Canadians and corporations

whose contributions of gifts-in-kind and funds have allowed the state rooms of Rideau Hall to be enhanced.

This book was published with the financial support of

CELANESE CANADA INC.

MR. JOSEPH SEGAL, C.M., O.B.C. AND MRS. ROSALIE SEGAL

MRS. GORDON T. SOUTHAM, C.M.

CONTENTS

III
GREENHOUSES, GARDENS AND GROUNDS

IV
BUILDING THE COLLECTION

PREFACE

When we were privileged to take up residence at Rideau Hall in January 1990, both of us were immediately struck by its beauty and moved by the deep historic significance this edifice has for all Canadians. We felt then, and believe even more strongly now, that Government House should represent the best of Canada — past and present — to visitors. It should be a source of pride and inspiration for all Canadians. Like residents before, our commitment is to not only maintain the building and grounds, but also to enhance it for future generations.

Since the first finely dressed stones were raised more than 150 years ago, age and use have taken their toll. Preservation and restoration of this precious legacy requires an ongoing effort. It was, therefore, most gratifying that a group of caring and generous Canadians interested in preserving their country's heritage formed Friends of Rideau Hall. With the cooperation and encouragement of the Canadiana Fund, the National Capital Commission and the Official Residences Council, these friends are now actively assisting in the further development of an outstanding national collection of art and furnishings.

While many thousands of Canadians visit Rideau Hall annually, both for official functions as well as public events and tours, we hope to extend the experience to citizens across the country — and friends around the world — through the words and images recorded in this book, proceeds from which will aid Friends of Rideau Hall in expanding the collection.

Welcome to our national home.

Ramon John Hnatyshyn

Gerda Hnatyshyn

Winter 1994

The front gate of Rideau Hall was re-opened to the public in 1990.

x

Each year, more than 45,000 visitors enjoy the gardens and parkland of Rideau Hall.

INTRODUCTION

"We are inclined to take Government House for granted. We think of it as an old house where the Governor General lives... actually it is Canada's most historic residence. Physically parts of it go back to the very beginnings of the community, and as the home of every Governor General since Confederation it has associations with our national story such as no other building in this country can boast."

[unidentified newspaper clipping dated October 14, 1935; National Archives of Canada, RG 11, vol. 4267, file 2134-14B.]

The possibility that his sprawling estate would one day become a vice-regal residence probably never occurred to Thomas MacKay. He was a Scottish stonemason who came to Canada and made his fortune building the Lachine and Rideau Canals, as well as mills on the Rideau Falls[1]. He had Rideau Hall built not far from the falls in 1838, and one of the streets bordering this residence is named after him. The original Rideau Hall, nucleus of the present official residence, was a rectangular, two-storey stone villa with a semi-circular front facing the garden.

In 1865, the house was leased to the government as a residence for Lord Monck, the 21st Governor General of British North America (and later the first Governor General of Canada). From that point on the house began to expand to provide more office and living space. Its floor area has grown to over 8,360 square metres. Thus, Rideau Hall became Government House, the name given throughout the British Empire to the residence and offices of vice-regal governors.

In 1868, the house and grounds were purchased by the Government of Canada. The complex of house, park and gardens lies roughly three kilometres north of the Parliament Buildings. The first Governor General travelled by boat to Parliament Hill. Today, the estate is usually approached by visiting heads of state and foreign dignitaries along Sussex Drive, on what is called Confederation Boulevard.

This ceremonial route is a symbolic link between Parliament at one end and the Crown at the other. Confederation Boulevard may be likened to the Champs Élysées, Pennsylvania Avenue or The Mall, in that there face upon it many edifices of government, the arts and the international community. The residence of the Prime Minister is located here. "Earnscliffe," once the home of Sir John A. Macdonald, Canada's first Prime Minister, is now occupied by the British High Commissioner. The embassies of France and Japan and the High Commission for South Africa are soon to be joined on this route by the new embassy of The United States of America.

---

[1] Rideau is a French word meaning 'curtain.' The Rideau Falls resemble a curtain of water. Thomas MacKay doubtless named his mansion after the nearby falls or the river that drops over them into the Ottawa River.

Visiting foreign dignitaries are often housed at No. 7 Rideau Gate, opposite the Prime Minister's residence and the gates of Rideau Hall. This was once the Lambart residence, also known as "Vine Lynne," named after the original owner's ancestral estate in England.

Government House has been the official residence of 24 governors general. Set in 31.7 hectares of trees, grass and gardens surrounded by the neighbourhoods of New Edinburgh, Lindenlea and the Village of Rockcliffe Park, it has been transformed from what was once a picturesque Regency villa into a majestic building. Splendidly situated in the centre of the city, the mansion reflects the aspirations of the Victorian era to formality and grandeur.

As Canada evolved, so did Rideau Hall. Changes were wrought by the people who lived and worked here; all were committed to enhancing it. Some rooms have been restored to their earlier state, and the residence has begun to convey its own history. At the same time, the house must always respond to new demands.

This building must not only function as the residence of the Governor General of Canada and his or her family, but also must be sufficiently flexible to host dignitaries and foreign heads of state one day and perhaps a garden party the next. Restricted public budgets mean innovative ways have to be found to maximize other resources. In the past, many Canadians have been very generous with their assistance. Now in this elegant setting, paintings, sculpture and decorative detail tell the story of Canada.

After more than 150 years of change, Rideau Hall appears remarkably coordinated and attractive. Government House in Ottawa is a happy blend of the formality befitting the functions it must serve and a warmth of hospitable understatement that is uniquely Canadian.

This book is a story of special relationships, friendships and achievements. It is also a tribute to the Canadians who have left their own distinctive mark on Government House. But in addition, it celebrates our country's proud history by inviting the reader to come into Rideau Hall to share this heritage

3

The impressive Ceremonial Guard at the front gate to Rideau Hall.

4

Governor General Roland Michener
undertook that Rideau Hall would be
"a neutral and friendly environment for
the discussion of differing points of
view, and a centre for the encourage-
ment of excellence in all worthy fields of
Canadian endeavour." [on the occasion
of his installation as Governor General,
April 17, 1967.]

The significance of Rideau Hall in national life is more clearly defined if there is an understanding of the role and the responsibilities of the Governor General who lives there. The Office of the Governor General bears a number of responsibilities both constitutional and traditional in nature. These relate to five major themes: the Crown in Canada, Canadian sovereignty, recognition of excellence, national identity and unity, and moral leadership.

A closer look at what these themes entail will reveal many of the important events in our national life which take place at Rideau Hall.

I

FOCAL

POINT OF

THE

NATION

In 1867 the British Parliament passed the *British North America Act*, the founding document of Canada as an independent nation. Drafted by Canadians who subsequently became known as the Fathers of Confederation, the document stated that "The Executive Government and Authority of and over Canada is hereby declared to continue and be vested in the Queen."

The *Constitution Act of 1982* provided, for the first time in our country's history, a way of amending the Constitution without having to obtain the approval of the British Parliament. This Act did not alter the status of Queen Elizabeth II as head of state in Canada. Her official representative in Canada is the Governor General.

There is a clear separation of roles between the head of state and the head of government. The Governor General is appointed by the Queen on the advice of the Prime Minister of Canada. Canada's head of government is the Prime Minister, a member of Parliament.

Whereas in the United States the President is both head of state and head of government, our Canadian system separates the functions so that the head of state can represent the citizens beyond the political exigencies of the head of government.

By constitutional convention, the Governor General has the right to be consulted, to encourage and to warn. One of the Governor General's many responsibilities is to ensure that Canada always has a prime minister. Should this position become vacant through death, resignation, parliamentary stalemate or party dissension, the Governor General must identify a replacement.

The Governor General gives royal assent to bills passed by the House of Commons and the Senate, thereby establishing the bills as Acts of Parliament (the laws of Canada). The Governor General also summons, prorogues and dissolves Parliament; delivers the Speech from the Throne at the opening of sessions, outlining the government's plans for legislation; signs state documents such as orders-in-council, commissions and pardons; and presides over the swearing-in of the Prime Minister and Cabinet, the Chief Justice and other members of the Privy Council, and the Chief of the Defence Staff.

The Canadian Coat of Arms (opposite).
The 20th Prime Minister of Canada taking the Oath of Office with the 26th Ministry in the Ballroom at Rideau Hall (left).
The Governor General delivers the Speech from the Throne in the Senate of Canada on Parliament Hill (overleaf).

7

The Governor General receives representatives of Commonwealth and other foreign states, who present themselves at Rideau Hall with Letters of Commission or Credence. The letters indicate that the High Commissioner or Ambassador is the accredited representative of his or her head of state with authority to speak in dealings with the Government of Canada. The Governor General's state visits to foreign countries are an important instrument of Canadian foreign policy and an effective way of fostering economic, cultural, industrial and humanitarian programmes.

The Governor General is also Commander-in-Chief of the Canadian Armed Forces. As such, he or she carries out a number of ceremonial military duties, many of which take place at Rideau Hall.

A most meaningful and agreeable duty of the Governor General, and one that brings many people to Rideau Hall, is the conferring of honours. In the national context, "honours" are defined as orders, decorations and medals granted or awarded by the Governor General on behalf of the Queen. They are symbols of excellence, recognizing significant achievements and conspicuous service.

Honours represent the highest accolades Canada can bestow and are a strong force in building a national sense of pride.

The ceremonial arrival of the President of Argentina and his daughter in an historic landau. Built in Australia in 1900, the vehicle was purchased by Earl Grey and brought to Canada when he became Governor General in 1904 (left top). Letters of Credence being presented by the Ambassador of Korea (left), and the Ambassador of Denmark (above top); Letter of Commission being presented by the High Commissioner of Mauritius (above).

On July 1, 1967, on the occasion of the Centennial of Confederation, the **Order of Canada** was established as the centrepiece of the Canadian Honours System. It pays tribute to Canadians who exemplify the highest qualities of citizenship and whose contributions enrich the lives of their contemporaries. It is awarded at three levels – Companion,

12 Officer and Member – for outstanding achievement and merit in service to Canada; to humanity at large; or to a particular locality, group, or field of activity.

The same levels or degrees apply to the **Order of Military Merit**, established in 1972, honouring outstanding fulfilment of responsibilities and exceptional service.

As Chancellor and Principal Companion of the Order of Canada and Chancellor of the Order of Military Merit, the Governor General presents the insignia to recipients at investiture ceremonies held at one of the two official residences: Rideau Hall in Ottawa and at La Citadelle in Québec.

The Insignia of Companion of the Order of Canada is composed of a stylized snowflake and maple leaf, representing Canada, and a Royal Crown, symbolizing the Sovereign as the fount of Canadian honours (above).
The Order of Canada ceremony is held in the Ballroom at Rideau Hall (right).

The Governor General is the Prior for Canada of the **Most Venerable Order of the Hospital of St. John of Jerusalem**. He presides at their investitures on behalf of Her Majesty the Queen. The **Royal Victorian Order** is a personal gift of Her Majesty for services rendered and is also part of the national honours available to Canadians.

Decorations recognize bravery, professionalism and exceptional devotion to duty and, unlike orders, may be awarded posthumously.

The Cross of Valour is Canada's highest decoration for bravery (above top).
The Insignia of Commander, Order of Military Merit (above).

The Canadian Honours System was enlarged in 1972 to comprise three decorations for bravery: the **Cross of Valour**, the **Star of Courage** and the **Medal of Bravery**, awarded for acts of conspicuous courage and bravery in perilous circumstances. The Canadian Decorations Advisory Committee for Bravery recommends to the Governor General the names of those who merit these marks of distinction. To these decorations was added the **Governor General's Commendation.**

In 1993, a series of decorations for military valour was approved by Her Majesty Queen Elizabeth II as part of the Canadian Honours System. These include the **Victoria Cross**, the **Star of Military Valour** and the **Medal of Military Valour.** They are awarded only in wartime by the Governor General on the advice of the Military Valour Advisory Committee.

The **Victoria Cross** was created by Queen Victoria in 1856 and was awarded to Canadians in all wars until 1945. The **Canadian Victoria Cross** retains the same design and the same awarding criteria as the **British Victoria Cross.** It is granted "for the most conspicuous bravery, a daring or pre-eminent act of valour or self-sacrifice or extreme devotion to duty, in the presence of the enemy." It is the highest in the order of precedence of Canadian honours.

The **Star** and **Medal of Military Valour** also recognize valiant service and devotion to duty in the presence of the enemy.

The **Meritorious Service Cross** and the **Meritorious Service Medal** have a civilian as well as a military division and are awarded for the performance of deeds or activities in an outstandingly professional manner or of a very high standard.

One of the youngest recipients of Canada's Medal of Bravery (above).
The investiture of the Order of St. John being held at the Notre Dame Basilica, located along the ceremonial route (right).

14

The *Governor General's Academic Medal* is awarded to those who achieve the highest academic marks in all levels of study from secondary to post-graduate. In addition, more than 50 scholarships, prizes and trophies are awarded in the name of the Governor General for outstanding achievements in fields ranging from the arts, science and engineering to good citizenship, humanities and sport. In most instances, these honours and awards bear the name of the governor general in whose name they are given.

A runner en route to the 1994 Commonwealth Games in Victoria, British Columbia, presents the Queen's Baton to the Governor General (above top).
Earl Grey contributed the Grey Cup, awarded to the winning team in the Canadian Football League (above left).

The Stanley Cup, presented annually to the top team in Canada's National Hockey League, was established by Lord Stanley (above right).

Familiar among these are the *Stanley Cup* for hockey and the *Grey Cup* for football. Others are:

the Governor General's Literary Awards, instituted by Lord Tweedsmuir

the Athlone-Vanier Engineering Fellowship

the Massey Medal for outstanding personal achievement in the exploration, development and description of geography of Canada

the Vanier Awards for Outstanding Young Canadians, presented annually to five Canadians between the ages of 18 and 40

the Michener Awards for Journalism for outstanding public service to the media

the Jules Léger Scholarship for scholastic achievement in bilingual programs

the Edward Schreyer Fellowship in Ukrainian Studies for post-doctoral research.

During the Hnatyshyn mandate, a further number of annual national awards were initiated, including scholarships in Environmental Science and Engineering and awards for lifetime achievements in Law, in Literacy and in the Performing Arts. The *Ramon John Hnatyshyn Scholarship* is offered in *Environmental and Canadian Studies.*

A nation that wishes to foster a sense of national pride encourages the development and use of symbols of sovereignty, community, family life and individual achievement.

To this end, the **Canadian Heraldic Authority** was established on

June 4, 1988, within the Office of the Governor General. By the creation of this new authority, Canada recognized the important part that heraldic symbols have played in fostering the Canadian identity and in visually dramatizing our history, geography and aspirations.

Canada was the first Commonwealth country outside the United Kingdom to establish its own heraldic authority. The Authority provides an indigenous mechanism for granting new coats of arms to Canadian communities, corporations, associations and individuals. It also offers a unique way of honouring the symbols of

Canada's native peoples and ethnic groups and a method of recording the hundreds of historically and artistically important heraldic symbols that form part of our Canadian heritage

The Chief Herald of Canada discusses heraldic designs with the artist, who is referred to as the Fraser Herald (above top). The heraldic insignia for the Chief Herald's Office (above).

17

PERFORMING ARTS

In the midst of a lavish show, before a sea of tuxedos and gowns that washed right up against the back wall of a National Arts Centre, host and actor Donald Sutherland recalled with a single homely remark what the Governor General's Performing Arts Awards are for.

"This," he said, "is to give us insight into the kind of person a country like ours can produce."

The major (and spoken) purpose of the awards is to redress our well-known national tendency to neglect our greatest artists. The participants were honoured with a live show involving some hundreds of singers, dancers and musicians. The winners were each the subject of spoken homage followed by a brief film about their lives, followed by a live performance.

The NAC lobby, awash in massive bouquets of white lilies and roses, was only slightly less splendid than the scarlet tunics of the military trumpeters who summoned the revellers into the concert hall.

[Ray Conlogue, The Globe and Mail
November 29, 1993.]

The Governor General's Performing Arts Award for Outstanding Achievement in Theatre is presented at Rideau Hall (top).
The Gala is held in the National Arts Centre (right).
The symbol for the Governor General's Performing Arts Awards (far right).
The awards are presented in five areas: theatre, dance, classical music and opera, popular music, and film and broadcasting (opposite).

18

✳

Large numbers of people come to Rideau Hall annually. In summer, guided tours of the house and grounds attract Canadians from across the country as well as many foreign visitors.

The Governor General receives the public twice a year. The annual New Year's Levee originated with the first governors (who then represented the Kings of France) who received citizens and wished a Happy New Year to all who presented themselves at the Château St-Louis, Québec. The first recorded New Year's Levee in Canada was held in 1646 under Charles de Montmagny. The custom was later adopted by the British governors. These days, the Levee begins at mid-morning, continuing until late afternoon. It provides an opportunity for representatives of the Canadian Order of Precedence, the diplomatic corps, parliamentarians, members of the Canadian Forces and the Royal Canadian Mounted Police, as well as the general public to wish the representative of the Crown a Happy New Year.

The Governor General also invites the public to a summer garden party at Rideau Hall – a very large affair.

✳

A nation needs a symbol to embody the spirit of the country. The Governor General effects this in part through association with a wide variety of organizations that are representative of the mosaic of the country. The Governor General is Chief Scout of Canada and patron of many organizations and events✳

Thousands of visitors take guided tours of Rideau Hall's greenhouses and grounds each year (above).
The façade of the Governor General's residence in autumn (right).

When in 1893 it was announced that Aberdeen would be Governor General, Lady Aberdeen sought Lady Derby's advice on the house. The latter replied: "You will find the furniture in the rooms very old-fashioned & not very pretty, but it is a comfortable house..... The walls are absolutely bare..... The room which has always been the wife of the G.G.'s sitting room is very empty..... There are no lamps in the house at all. No cushions...in fact none of the small things that make a room pretty & comfortable."

Governor General Vincent Massey thought that as a piece of architecture Rideau Hall might be regarded as possessing a certain lovable eccentricity, but it also had a welcoming atmosphere despite the presence of some of the most regrettable pieces of furniture he had ever seen.

Such is the story of Rideau Hall: the handing on of a barely furnished house from one family to another, the character of the house consequently changing with the people. Yet... something was always left behind in house or grounds to mark each occupancy. More importantly, each family left in perpetuity to Canada some legacy, achievement, tradition or germinal idea.

[R.H. Hubbard: Rideau Hall]

The ornate iron gates of Rideau Hall still survive and stand open during the day. In summer, in daylight hours, a fountain in front of the porte-cochère. The "Fountain of Hope" was given in the International Year for Disabled Persons

II

INSIDE

THE HOUSE

Front Entrance

First Floor

A Front Entrance Hall
B Ambassadors' Room
C Reception Room
D Tent Room
E Long Gallery
F Verandah
G Ballroom
H Canadian Room

I First-floor Corridor
J Drawing Room
K Small Drawing Room
L Dining Room
M Small Dining Room
N Library
O Spouse's Study
P Governor General's Study

the Ceremonial Guard attracts the attention of the thousands of tourists who come to visit and photograph this historic house.

The driveway, which was laid out during Lord Monck's tenure, meanders slightly uphill along an allée of large oaks and maples and curves around by the Canadian Football League to perpetuate the spirit of the gallant young Canadian hero, Terry Fox.

There is a warm welcome at Rideau Hall for every visitor, whether a dignitary from another country or a member of a tour group. This is a friendly place.

Fountain of Hope (above).
Front Entrance Hall (opposite).

FRONT ENTRANCE HALL

On entering, the visitor is immediately
made aware of the status of the residence
in Canada's history. There are two
panels which display the names and
the coats of arms of all governors and
governors general since 1608. They
visually represent the chronology of
Canada through heraldic artwork and
the names which have become so
familiar to Canadians.

*A bust of the Marquess of Lorne (fourth Governor General
of Canada) was completed in 1879 by Princess Louise's friend,
Henrietta Montalba (above).*
*Entrance Hall panels display the coats of arms of governors and
governors general since 1608. Revealed through the archway is
the official portrait of Canada's 23rd Governor General,
Jeanne Sauvé (right).*

Your attention will be directed to two magnificent stained-glass windows with armorial bearings, designed by Canadian artist Christopher Wallis, and unveiled by Her Majesty Elizabeth II, Queen of Canada, in 1992. Hamilton and Marion Southam donated the window that explains in symbols the role of the monarchy in our country. Their Excellencies, Governor General and Mrs. Hnatyshyn, donated the other, which represents the seven Canadian mandates.

The neo-classical-style Entrance Hall, characterized by grace and symmetry, has retained all of its original architectural features, notably the marble wainscoting, the staircase and the coffered ceiling. The four royal portraits adorning the walls, all copies of originals by British artists, are of King Edward VII, Queen Alexandra, King George VI and his consort Queen Elizabeth (now Queen Elizabeth The Queen Mother).

Provincial and territorial flags are draped on one wall. On adjoining walls hang the Colours of the illustrious Queen's and Canadian guards.

The large Jacobean-style hall settee is part of the Molson-Macpherson Collection, a gift to Rideau Hall in the 1930s. Two hall benches in Gothic revival style date from the 1860s.

On a sunny day, when light streams in through the stained-glass windows and plays off the glass and

brass of the doors, the whole hall is an explosion of colour ✤

The royal window commemorates the 40th anniversary of the accession to the Throne of Her Majesty Queen Elizabeth (above).
A symbol celebrating the 125th anniversary of Confederation (right).
The vice-regal window commemorates the 40th anniversary of the appointment of Canadian-born governors general and the 25th anniversary of the Canadian Honours System (opposite).

AMBASSADORS' ROOM

A billiard room until the late 1920s, this space then served as an anteroom where ambassadors and their guests were occasionally received. Now decorated in contemporary style, this room has been used since 1990 to display exhibits, such as Canadian honours and heraldry, associated with the role of the Office of the Governor General 🎖

Exhibits such as the Canadian Honours System are of interest to visitors of all ages. During May and June, hundreds of school children tour the Ambassadors' Room (above and right).

RECEPTION ROOM

Here, in 1838, Thomas and Anne MacKay would have welcomed guests to their new Regency villa. Perhaps Thomas played his bagpipes.

Today, the room is sufficiently flexible to be used for formal events, receiving lines, buffets and photo opportunities for the media, and also

for ceremonies involving limited numbers of people.

The rope mouldings of the door surrounds are a distinctive feature. On the walls are portraits of former Canadian governors general. Perhaps the most forceful portraits are those of Jeanne Sauvé by Cleeve Horne and of Jules and Gabrielle Léger by Jean-Paul Lemieux.

The official portrait of the Légers was painted by Québec artist Jean-Paul Lemieux (above).

Also in the room are portraits of governors general Massey, by L.T. Newton, Vanier and Michener by Charles Comfort and Schreyer by Helen Parsons Shepherd.

Among many fine pieces of furniture and objets d'art – gifts to the Crown – are two oak refectory tables, one of them 17th century, donated to Rideau Hall by Geoffrey Lynch-Staunton of Québec. Well displayed is Inuit artist Moses Aupuluktuk's soapstone sculpture, which was a gift to Mrs. Norah Michener.

A pair of lacquer armchairs in Italian Renaissance revival style, a gift from the Molson-Macpherson Collection, grace the ensemble.

29

30

In 1975, the lieutenant governors of the provinces gave the Légers a handsome lectern which, in turn, was left to Government House.

On a sideboard sit a pair of silver pilgrim bottles given to King George V which have been on loan from Buckingham Palace since the 1960s.

The unique, pear-shaped design is reminiscent of water vessels seen in ancient Rome. Since the 17th century, they have become decorative objects

The official portrait of the Right Hon. Edward Schreyer was painted by H. Parsons Shepherd of Newfoundland (above top). One of a pair of pilgrim bottles. They were a wedding gift to the Duke of York from his grandmother, Queen Victoria (above). The Reception Room (right).

Official portraits of the Right Hon. Vincent Massey by artist Lilias Torrance Newton (top), the Right Hon. Georges Vanier (centre) and the Right Hon. Roland Michener both by Charles Comfort.

Sparkling silver, seasonal flowers and an array of culinary delights are impeccably positioned for an Order of Canada buffet.

TENT ROOM

The distinct character of this unique space makes it one of the most intriguing rooms in the house. Originally it was

With the exception of the Willingdon era, the walls have always featured red- and white-striped awnings. In 1988, following a total rehabilitation

of the structure, a committee chaired by the Right Honourable Jeanne Sauvé oversaw the completion of the interior design.

built as a tennis court during the Dufferin residency to balance the Ballroom built on the north side. It is a far cry from the wooden edifice in which, in the early hours of March 23, 1876, 1500 guests of Lord and Lady Dufferin dined, following a fancy-dress ball. Their Excellencies appeared as King James of Scotland and his Queen.

Here one finds a shift in texture from the painted surfaces of the rest of the building. The splendid refurbishing features an elegant marriage of mirrored

A special reception was held to honour the athletes who represented Canada at the 1994 Winter Olympic Games in Norway (above).
The British Columbian artists who designed the Queen's Baton for the 1994 Commonwealth Games meet with the Governor General. The Queen's Baton is the Commonwealth Games equivalent of the Olympic Torch (left).
The Tent Room in readiness (overleaf).

doors with blue- and coral-striped awnings and walls. The fabric, the brass and glass chandeliers, and the mahogany pier tables and cabinets are all made in Canada. The black-and-white Carrera marble "carpet" conveys a sense of increased scale as well as a feeling of coolness and grandeur. A new addition is the minstrels' gallery, which can accommodate musicians or the media. The walls are hung with portraits of former British governors general

Each year since the 1950s, members of the Ottawa Boys and Girls Club and Le Patro have been invited to a Christmas party at Rideau Hall.

LONG GALLERY

Lady Willingdon was by now, in her husband's words, "knocking this old house about in such a way that it must be getting the shock of its life." Like many another wife before her, she had found it in urgent need of her attentions. From the very first day she was shifting furniture so furiously that the ADCs had to make detours through back passages in order to avoid being caught by her and pressed into service.

[R.H. Hubbard: Rideau Hall]

Princess Alice, Countess of Athlone: "I set to work. Government House was excellent, but, as usual, I turned all the furniture upside down to suit my taste. We moved the whole of the furniture in the Long Gallery, where every chair and sofa were up against the wall, and made three 'encampments' so that you could sit and talk in groups and feel more comfortable. It was really quite a nice room when we had done with it."

37

The name "Long Gallery" conjures up images of English manor houses, centuries old and filled with family history and precious works of art. Rideau Hall's Long Gallery is not all of this, but yet, in its 80-year period of existence, the room has developed an interesting history, blending and harmonizing a collection of furnishings associated with it.

The Long Gallery was built in 1912, during the regime of the Duke and Duchess of Connaught, at a time when major alterations were being undertaken to add more dignity to the residence.

Designed as a dining room and living space, the extra "parlour" was justified, given the increase in the number and type of social functions.

During the early years, the room was known as the Blue Gallery, but by far the most fascinating period in the Long Gallery's history was during the mandate of Lord Willingdon. Fresh from a stint in China and laden with treasures, Lady Willingdon transformed the room into an exotic Chinese gallery. The effect was so positive that it attracted the attention of *Canadian Homes and Gardens*.

Participants in a meeting of the Ontario Breast Cancer Screening Program gather for a reception in the Long Gallery (above). The elegant yet comfortable Long Gallery was recently restored. (overleaf).

On their departure, the
Willingdons sold their collection to
the government, and the oriental motif
survived for almost 20 years. The
Long Gallery then saw the addition of a
number of doorways connecting it to the
Tent Room, an enrichment of its ceiling
surfaces, and numerous decorative
schemes, each a reflection of its time.

Inasmuch as many of the
pieces from the Willingdon period have
survived and have since been restored,
the Official Residences Council recently
proposed returning the decor of this
room to the Chinese period of the
late 1920s. A new oak floor was laid in
the autumn of 1991, and the ceiling
fixtures original to the room were
reinstated in 1993. Five custom-created
Chinese carpets, given to Rideau Hall
by the Hongkong Bank of Canada,

*The Straits Chinese porcelain bridal basin and plate are
decorated with phoenix and peonies. The late 19th-century
teacup with matching cover and saucer are from the K'ang-hse
(1662-1722) period (above).*

have become the focal point of several seating areas. One of these is a reproduction of an original from the Willingdon collection. The other four were custom designed, adapting the motifs and

painted in colour and gilt, and some were inlaid with mother-of-pearl. They add a crowning touch to the blue silk draperies. A Rococo gilt-wood mirror creates a striking visual accent on the far wall of

colours of the historical Chinese carpets of the same period. The seven eye-catching valances incorporate hand-carved panels from the late 19th-century Ching Dynasty period. These intricate carvings were originally

the Long Gallery. It is a mid-18th-century Chippendale pier glass, the gift of Mrs. F.M. Gaby, Toronto, in 1977.

The Long Gallery features several inviting niches that are naturally conducive to informal conversation (left). An exquisitely embroidered early 20th-century Chinese wedding gown was restored by the Canadian Conservation Institute (above).

The room's furnishings consist of antiques and original artifacts acquired over the many years. Many have been acquired through the Canadiana Fund[2] or donated by interested Canadians. For instance, the superb silk moiré upholstery fabric in a butterfly pattern on the four wing-back chairs was donated in 1992 by Mr. Budd Sugarman, Toronto.

Other items donated and placed in this room include an early 20th-century Chinese wedding gown, gift of Eva Lee Kwok, a Vancouver resident, and a mid-19th-century Chinese jardinière, gift of Agnes Benidickson, Ottawa. One of the most handsome pieces in the room is the sofa covered in blue silk damask, on loan from the Government of Nova Scotia.

The Long Gallery's warmth and intimacy is engendered by flashes of colour and by the grouping of the furniture. Potted palm trees emphasize the Victorian love of plants. Modern lampshades on the original fixtures create a sophisticated play of light. A rich glow of the Orient is captured forever in stunning simplicity. It exemplifies a remark by the great French couturière Madame Carven: *"Elegance resides in what you don't see. It shouldn't be grand; it should reveal itself little by little."*

43

[2] Established in March 1990 to assist in the furnishing of the seven official government residences, the Board has members from each province.

The black and gilt lacquer Chinese chest and screen (opposite), and the red lacquer Chinese armoire (above) were originally used in the Long Gallery by the Willingdons.

44

VERANDAH

The sunlit Verandah was once an open porch off the Long Gallery. Enclosed in the mid-1930s, it now provides a delightful informal gathering place for family and guests during four or five months of the year – when it is neither too hot nor too cold. Airy white wicker settees and chairs accented with colourful floral cushions create a garden-like atmosphere. A profusion of plants provides a natural progression from house to garden.

The room can seat up to 20 guests and is a vantage point for viewing a panorama of lush green and spring-blooming perennials. In the summer, two white marquees on either side of a central path stand ready to be used for receptions ❧

Luncheon is served in the Verandah to members of Ottawa's May Court Club (above).

BALLROOM

The Ballroom is a highlight of any tour of Rideau Hall. This largest and most formal state room in the residence is positively breathtaking. Constructed during the occupancy of the Dufferins, the Victorian architecture has been retained. The visitor is transported to a grand salon of la belle époque.

It was a daunting challenge to furnish a space in such exquisite, timeless taste. Pale turquoise silk draperies with gold trim are tied back, puddling to the floor in emulation of the richest Victorian window treatment. The area is anchored by a vast rug laid on rich herringbone oak.

The focal point is a central Waterford cut-glass chandelier of dimensions appropriately magnificent. It was presented to Rideau Hall on Victoria Day in 1951 by the British government

At the heart of the double-height Ballroom is a splendid neo-classical English-style chandelier (above right). An elaborately swagged French silk panel contributes to the Victorian decor of the room (above).

in gratitude for Canada's role in World War II. The turn-of-the-century Queen Anne style ballroom chairs are covered in opulent silk damask. Aesthetic unity is sustained by the recurrence of patterns and themes.

Opening into the Ballroom is an anteroom with a 19th-century English sofa, such as were designed to be placed under large paintings. Here a portrait of the young Queen Victoria in her coronation robes presides over the south side of the room, reflecting the era when the Ballroom was built. The oil is a copy by

J.H. Walker of a Sir George Hayter original. It was Queen Victoria who was responsible for choosing Ottawa as the nation's capital.

Pairs of original Rococo revival pier glasses made by the Toronto firm of Jacques and Hay still survive. The two fine late 19th-century Sèvres urns on gilded plinths were given by the Freiman family of Ottawa in honour of Mr. and Mrs. A.J. Freiman. Each presents a Napoleonic coronation scene on one side and a château landscape on the reverse.

Two windows in stained glass depict the performing arts and allude to the annual Governor General's Performing Arts Awards. They have been donated by the American Friends of Canada, Her Honour Mrs. Dorothy Lam, the Honourable Robert G. Rogers, O.C. and Mrs. E. Jane Rogers and Mr. Arthur and Mrs. Mary Shoults.

The Ballroom has long been used for entertaining. The entry in Lady Dufferin's diary on Tuesday, April 15, 1873, recorded its official opening – a ball. Because the ballroom was still unpainted, it was decorated with blue-and-white twists of tarlatan (muslin) and bunches of pink roses. The room was lit by 94 gas brackets.

The Ballroom was nearly three years old when, on Monday evening January 17, 1876, a play was being performed for a large children's party. Everything went well until near the end when, during a beautiful fairy transformation scene, the stage-hand attending to a limelight held a candle under a rubber gas pipe. The pipe melted and the gas burned furiously. Fire broke out. People rushed about, water flowed and great confusion ensued, but disaster was averted. Throughout the turmoil the imperturbable queen of the fairies kept her head and continued her speech.

Rounded shapes, integral to the Ballroom's architecture, are complemented by the form of the gilt-framed mirrors and opulently swagged and trimmed drapery (previous pages). Glenn Gould's concert piano (top).
Portraits of Her Majesty Queen Elizabeth II and His Royal Highness Prince Philip are by Lilias Torrance Newton (right).

A concert piano, formerly used for practice by the late Glenn Gould, stands in the alcove to one side. It was a gift for the Ballroom from the Government of Canada, requested by the Right Honourable Edward Schreyer and Mrs. Lily Schreyer. The eminent Canadian pianist Marc-André Hamelin used it for his recital here in 1992.

During the last decade, other guest artists have included The Orford String Quartet, dancer Annette av Paul, and for "Christmas at Rideau Hall," singers Louis and Gino Quilico. Such entertainments are often broadcast by the Canadian Broadcasting Corporation. Some formal ceremonies have also been televised in the Ballroom with the aid of discreetly placed lighting.

With candlelight glittering from the chandelier and the candelabra, one can almost hear the music and laughter of 19th-century soirées. The room is perfectly contrived for luxurious entertainment

Canadian athletes in the 1994 Special Olympics and Winter Olympics pose for an official photograph in the Ballroom (above top).
Architectural details, such as this gilt ceiling medallion, augment the stateliness of the Ballroom (above).

CANADIAN ROOM

The small Canadian Room is part of the original MacKay villa. In 1959, Madame Vanier wanted a room that reflected Canadian heritage. The space is comfortably furnished with Québec and Maritime antiques, such as the state areas, fits in beautifully with the rest of the decor.

Because of its simplicity and warmth, the Canadian Room is often used as a sitting room for holding informal meetings, and occasionally for media opportunities.

Louis XV Québec pine armoire which was acquired through the Canadiana Fund. It is remarkable for its strong decorative detail, especially the carved conch shells on the upper corners. A recently discovered turn-of-the-century Axminster carpet, originally used in the

As elsewhere in the house, generous donations are in evidence. One of the rarest Canadian pieces, a priceless gem, is a fauteuil à la capucine, the gift of Jacques Ouellet of Québec.

Armchairs à la capucine are considered to be Canada's most original and distinctive chairs. This one dates from the latter part of the 18th century (above).

A handcrafted New Brunswick cherry rocking chair by Steven Morgan was presented by the people of the province to the Hnatyshyns when they were on an official visit.

Many of the works of art have been acquired through the Canadiana Fund or Friends of Rideau Hall. Forty-one Alberta families gave a watercolour

portrait, painted by William Armstrong in 1906, of Crowfoot, Chief of the Blackfoot, who helped to preserve peace between his people and the builders of the Canadian Pacific Railroad.

Claude Picher answered a call for donations of Canadian art and gave three of his paintings, one of which is here. Above the fireplace is a wall tapestry

Warm shades of red and blue create a relaxing atmosphere in the Canadian Room (left).
Portrait of Chief Crowfoot by William Armstrong (above).

made around 1940, and on another wall is a small rug from Grenfell, Labrador, both hand-hooked and gifts of Mhairi de Castro in 1992. A pioneer woman prospector, Mrs. Viola MacMillan, presented an A.Y. Jackson oil.

Also contributing to the Canadian theme is a dining table of pine and maple with cabriole legs and a skirt

on all sides carved in os de mouton. Bookshelves provide storage for a growing collection of books that have won the Governor General's Literary Awards.

The Canadian Room reveals a delight in contrasting materials. It is a showcase of much that is fine in the decorative arts in Canada

A party of Korean guests prepares to attend an official ceremony (above).
The distinctive Grenfell rug is named after Dr. Wilfred Grenfell who organized a cottage industry of rug-makers along the remote northern coasts of Newfoundland and Labrador in the early part of this century (right).

FIRST-FLOOR CORRIDOR

In 1865, a long addition was added to the east side of the original MacKay villa in preparation for the occupancy of Viscount Monck who would become the first Governor General in 1867. This controversial step was expected to be a temporary measure; the house had been leased, not purchased. The architect planned the work "within as modest a sum as possible."

The typically Victorian narrow First-floor Corridor extends the entire length of the Monck wing, opening abruptly upon two original handsome staircases.

53

The coffered ceiling and richly hued carpet lead the eye down the corridor to the portrait of Lord Lansdowne (fifth Governor General of Canada).

Among the works of art to be found in the First-floor Corridor are portraits of Queen Victoria and Prince Albert, painted after Winterhalter in 1859, a gift of Princess Alice, Countess of Athlone; 17th-century antique maps, the gift of Bernard and Sylvia Ostry; an Emily Carr painting donated by Joan Chalmers, and four watercolour sketches of the Marquess of Lorne from Princess Louise's sketch-book, on loan from Dr. Naomi Jackson Groves.

A Riopelle oil, presented by the late Dr. R.H. Hubbard, hangs near the Canadian Room. Allen Sapp, a Cree artist from Saskatchewan, is represented in a 1978 gift to the Légers. The water-colours, *Scenes of Lévis, Québec*, painted by W.F. Friend in 1853, are part of the Official Residences Collection.

The imposing Royal Staircase, curving up from the corridor under a skylight, has been painted repeatedly over the years. A recent restoration has revealed the natural wood and fine turning on the stairs.

An attractive sideboard has been placed in the stairwell, fitting the location perfectly.

Portraits of Her Majesty Queen Victoria and His Royal Highness Prince Albert (above).
An elegantly furnished niche beneath the staircase features a mahogany sideboard and mid-19th-century watercolours,
Scenes of Lévis, Québec by W.F. Friend (right).

Handsome pieces of furniture are placed along the length of the First-floor Corridor. A mid-18th-century mahogany English tall-case clock is the work of Thomas Brass. Among the most important furnishings at Rideau Hall is another mahogany Regency piece, an excellent table, circa 1825, by Thomas Nisbet of St. John, New Brunswick, one of Canada's best-known master cabinet-makers. It features double astragals, rope mouldings and acanthus-carved legs, and was presented in 1978 by the Honourable Richard Hatfield, Premier of New Brunswick.

55

These elaborate console brackets are part of the original house.

A feature of grace and interest is a decorated Georgian six-panel door. Princess Louise, daughter of Queen Victoria and wife of the Marquess of Lorne, took brushes into hand in about 1880 to paint apple branches heavy with fruit on the door. In this work she was very much in tune with the flourishing Arts and Crafts Movement of her day. Originally facing into her boudoir, the essentially feminine decoration reveals the artist's taste. It is much admired and was featured on the Governor General's 1993 Christmas card.

The Thermadel Foundation and Margaret McCain donated a pair of Nisbet mahogany games tables. One stands adjacent to a George III mahogany-veneer breakfront bookcase, circa 1770, the gift of Dale and Dingwall of Toronto (left). A door decorated by Princess Louise (above).

Near the Royal Staircase is a majestic painting of Lady Aberdeen, an exemplary woman who was active in many phases of Canadian life. It was painted at Rideau Hall in 1898 by W.H. Funk and appropriately was given to Government House by the National Council of Women, an organization that Lady Aberdeen helped found.

A portrait of Lady Aberdeen (wife of the seventh Governor General of Canada) is placed, appropriately, over one of the chairs she originally donated to the Victorian Order of Nurses. The Victorian hall table is original to Rideau Hall (left). Such is my ability, an 18th-century painting by Johann Zoffany, was given to Lord Alexander (17th Governor General of Canada) by Sir James Dunn (above).

Alkali Slough, *an acrylic painting on canvas by Dorothy*
Knowles and a tall-case clock made in the early 19th century by
Twiss and Co. of Montréal, Québec, grace a spacious corner in
the corridor adjacent to the Canadian Room.

EMILY CARR

Hanging opposite Lady
Aberdeen is a portrait of Queen
Alexandra at the time of her marriage,
when she was Princess of Wales, painted
by F.X. Winterhalter. It is on loan from
the Royal Collection by gracious
permission of Her Majesty, along with
a portrait of Edward VII when Prince of
Wales, a work of the same artist 🏵

B.C. Forest *by Emily Carr (top).*
Lake Cinch Mine, Beaver Lodge,
Canada *by A.Y. Jackson (left).*

DRAWING ROOM

Originally furnished in the fashion of the
Victorian era, this room was used as
a tea or supper room. The appearance
remained basically the same throughout
the 19th century. In the early 1900s, the
room underwent a total transformation
to the neo-classical style of the 18th
century. Deep-swagged valances now
enhance the stately proportions of the
windows.

With sophistication added to
comfort – the two most coveted qualities
in a drawing room – this former family
parlour has become a living museum of
furniture and art, housing some of the
most important treasures in the collection, set like gems in the formal decor.

On the richly coloured and
intricately figured floor is a superb
antique Herez carpet donated by Gordon
and Jean Southam of Vancouver. Portraits
of some former Rideau Hall chatelaines
grace the room. Two are by Sir Philip
de Laszlo, one of the most renowned
English portrait artists of the early 20th
century. Lady Willingdon is represented
in her gift to Government House in 1931;
and the portrait of Madame Pauline
Vanier, painted in 1928, is on loan from
the National Gallery of Canada.
Princess Louise was painted by William
Richmond.

*A charming portrait of Princess Louise presides over the splendid
Georgian mantel (right).*
*An intricately patterned Herez carpet, made in northwestern
Persia in the late 19th century, lends a hint of the exotic to the
Drawing Room (opposite).*

62

The Duchess of Connaught keeps an eye on the best example of furniture that the family left to the Crown – a late 19th-century Carleton House desk in mahogany and satinwood, originally designed by the firm Gillow. Its history is evident in the impressed "C", indicating that this neo-classical piece once belonged to the Connaught family.

A portrait of Lady Willingdon is placed above an 18th-century English serpentine chest, part of the Ostry Collection (opposite). Madame Vanier's portrait hangs above a late 19th-century writing table made for the Prince of Wales, later King George IV, when he resided at Carleton House. The original desk design, by Gillow, circa 1796 (above).

Today, this parlour is regularly the setting for cultural, social and state functions. It has been used for the swearing-in of government ministers when there are only individual changes to the Cabinet, for the formal gathering of guests before and after dinners, and for receiving heads of state. Presentation of Easter and Christmas seals to Their Excellencies by young Canadians may be made here, and the annual tea for the Silver Cross Mother and youth representatives on Remembrance Day is held in this room 🦁

67

Princess Louise of Prussia, The Duchess of Connaught, *by F.M. Skipworth, after a portrait by John Singer Sargent (opposite).*
A mahogany escritoire in the English neo-classical style, circa 1900, displays commemorative silverware from the Vincent Massey Collection, donated by his son, Hart Massey, through the Canadiana Fund (left).
A reception for the Governor General's Performing Arts Awards was held in the room in 1993 (above).

SMALL DRAWING ROOM

The *Petit Salon* once served as a library. Later it became a private tea room, probably because of its size. More recently, it was transformed into a comfortable sitting room furnished in the classical manner. It offers an intimate setting when the Drawing Room would be too grand. The seating is plump and comfortable. The colour scheme of bright yellows and burgundy has irresistible charm.

68

Foreign guests, visiting dignitaries or political leaders wait here to be received by the Governor General. When the Queen is in Ottawa, Her Majesty holds private audiences in these intimate surroundings 🦁

A pair of birch armchairs are decorated with early Georgian foliage modified by the graceful curved lines typical of art nouveau. The Edwardian firescreen, circa 1900, has a carved and gilt frame enclosing an oriental silk panel (right). A detail of a finely carved mantel shows its distinctly Georgian style (above).

Madame Anna Biolik

DINING ROOM

The gracious setting of the Dining Room is perfect for formal and elegant entertaining. Three 20th-century crystal

This menu is inspired by the earliest recorded dinner given on the occasion of an installation of a Governor General of Canada. The dinner was offered in honour of the Marquess of Lorne and the Princess Louise on November 30, 1878

chandeliers illuminate the table settings, giving a lively warmth to the fine furniture and silver.

Exquisitely woven Pratesi linens are the perfect backdrop for the Limoges state china selected by Madame Vanier. The menu for this particular banquet, the 1990 installation of the present Governor General, was inspired by the first recorded menu at Rideau Hall for the installation of the Marquess of Lorne (left and above).
A calligrapher produces a draft of the menu used for the installation (above and top right).
The finishing flourish to the 1990 installation banquet was served on specially designed Royal Worcester Spode china (right).

The mahogany banquet table dates from the mid-1960s. Its adjustable design allows for seating up to 40 guests. The traditional Chippendale side chairs date from the regime of the Duke of Connaught.

The sterling silver on permanent display was graciously loaned by Buckingham Palace. A mahogany English-style breakfront features a collection of dinnerware used at the residence throughout the years.

Portraits of Princess Louise and her cousin, Princess Helena, adorn the walls. Both are by Georg Koberwein and are copies after F.X. Winterhalter. The paintings are gifts of Princess Alice, Countess of Athlone. All other portraits in the Dining Room are from the Official Residences Collection, including one of the Duke of Richmond, a copy after John Hopper

Rideau Hall staff pay meticulous attention to the most minute details of the dining room set-up. The mahogany table seats 40 (previous pages).
In 1979, special Royal Worcester Spode china was designed featuring the insignia of the Order of Canada (above left).
The gracious arrangement of Princess Louise's portrait, flowers in a silver pierced basket and tiered bonbonnières contribute to the elegance of the Dining Room (above).

A formal luncheon for the advisory board of the Order of
Canada (above right).
The long mahogany sideboard, dating from the mid-19th
century, is said to be one of the surviving pieces from the
MacKay villa (right).

SMALL DINING ROOM

This room is joined to its neighbour, the Library, by back-to-back fireplaces in the centre of the rooms, framed on each side by archways. New shutters allow the northern light to suffuse the delicate pastel walls. Now used for official luncheons and dinners, this once served as a bedroom and dressing room for Lady Monck and as a study for the Earl of Aberdeen.

The small dining area features a double-pedestal mahogany table surrounded by 13 Chippendale chairs. The original leather of the seats bears a delicate patina. The chairs, which had belonged to Lord and Lady Aberdeen, were for many years in the boardroom of the Victorian Order of Nurses in Ottawa.

The works of art in this room include a René Richard painting, a gift to the Légers, and a porcelain collection designed and hand-painted in 1919 by Alice Egan Hagen of Halifax, Nova Scotia. The latter was presented by the daughter of the artist in 1984

Dazzling morning sunlight brings the Small Dining Room to glittering life.

76

A door leading to Lady Monck's dressing room was converted into a cupboard. The china is a selection of items from a 43-piece French porcelain tea service hand-decorated with the flags and pictures representing the Allied countries in World War I by Nova Scotia artist Alice Egan Hagen.

THE LIBRARY

The Library is a mellow, informal room conducive to conversation or study. It has been a favourite retreat of previous occupants and guests alike. Originally, it was the study of the Marquess of Lorne, and later was a boudoir for both Lady Stanley and Lady Aberdeen.

The Library houses a modest, but growing collection of first-edition Canadian books, in both official languages. They are displayed on modern shelving designed for this room. Vincent Massey's partners' desk has found its perfect setting.

The Library features a fine selection of furniture including a pair of Gainsborough armchairs, circa 1760, and the Regency metamorphic armchair/library steps, circa 1820, from the Ostry Collection (opposite).
This room is both an informal retreat and a convenient reference centre for residents and guests (above).

A pair of 18th-century Gainsborough library chairs have recently been acquired through the Friends of Rideau Hall. They represent the company's fine standards of chair making. Sir Joshua Reynolds' portrait of Lord Amherst, above the fireplace, was a gift from the estate of H.R. MacMillan. The curio table with its neo-classical Chippendale motifs dates from circa 1900 and is part of the Connaught Collection. It is used for displaying rare books. A bronze sculpture by Susan Stromberg-Stein is a gift of the artist.

80

A superbly preserved example of a turn-of-the-century Herez carpet is a gift of The W. Garfield Weston Foundation

The finish on Vincent Massey's desk is complemented by the strong pattern and colours in the Herez carpet. In front of the desk sits a George III mahogany tub chair with a horseshoe back rest and serpentine seat, circa 1830 (right). Bronze sculpture of a violinist (opposite).

81

CHATELAINE'S STUDY

Upon entering this room, the eye is immediately drawn to an intricately patterned ceiling cornice, a remnant of the high Victorian enrichments which resulted when plasterers were offered ample opportunities to demonstrate their skills.

Here one finds the 19th century mingled with the distinctively modern. The ambience is cool, calm and eclectic. Glorious light streams in through tall, handsomely shuttered windows, even on the gloomiest of days. The vista of the private formal garden is breathtaking.

When Lady Willingdon used the room, it had cushions of "the favoured purple," a purple leather desk set and mauve chrysanthemums. The fashionable mauve appeared on everything from her writing paper to the exterior of the vice-regal railway carriages.

Citizens concerned about breast cancer awareness meet in the Chatelaine's Study (right).
The delicate plaster garland encircling the ceiling is part of the original house dating from 1865 (above).

So thorough was Lady Willingdon's application of this colour that it took a long time to fade from prominence. Today, there is little evidence of her trail of mauve except for some of the original Willingdon chairs still in use here.

A comfortable sofa and chairs are oriented around a work table to create a meeting place. Most of the books and artwork are from the occupants' private collection 🍁

Her Excellency consults with the staff designer about the ongoing historical restoration projects (above top).
Her Excellency's cameo motif is adapted from the Hnatyshyn's Coats of Arms. The maple leaf symbolizes Canada and the Vice-Regal Office while the heart, representing her family's heritage, is from the Danish Coat of Arms (above).

GOVERNOR GENERAL'S STUDY

Built after the turn of the century during the incumbency of Lord Minto and displacing an earlier greenhouse, the round tower containing the Governor General's Study on the first floor was designed to complement the lines of the original MacKay villa at the other end of the south front. The curved space within, with its oak panelling, is warm and inviting. The large windows overlooking the private terrace are shaded in summer by the large maples that dominate the west lawn.

Over the fireplace is an ornately carved panel with the Royal Arms, while other oak panels around the room bear the names of governors general since Confederation.

Most of the furniture in this room is part of a major collection donated to Rideau Hall by Bernard and Sylvia Ostry. It includes a Regency mahogany pedestal draughtsman's desk with gilt ornamental fittings and an inset tooled-leather top.

Personal accents in this room include the reading materials and the fancied echoes of past occupants.

It is in this study overlooking the gardens that the governors general of this century have conducted the affairs of state.

It was here, in 1926, that Lord Byng had a strained meeting with Prime Minister Mackenzie King when the Governor General refused to dissolve Parliament for the second time in nine months. It was here too, that Lord Bessborough inaugurated the Trans-Canada telephone service by speaking with each of the lieutenant governors. And it was here in this study, in February 1949, that Lord Alexander signed the Terms of Union that brought Newfoundland into Canada.

Until 1941, the Governor General also used an office in the East Block on Parliament Hill. Today, this office is still used by the Queen or the Governor General on ceremonial occasions

The Governor General meets with representatives of the Boy Scouts of Canada (Les Scouts) in his study (left).
A detail of the Royal Arms carved in the oak mantelpiece (above).
The Governor General's shield motif is adapted from the Hnatyshyns' Coats of Arms (right).
The focal point of the Governor General's Study is the 19th-century Regency draughtsman's desk (overleaf).

$\mathcal{U}$pstairs, a spacious hall corresponds to the First-floor Corridor and provides access to state guest rooms, the Royal Suite, the Chapel and the private quarters which lie beyond the double doors of the Minto Wing.

Built-in closets are being replaced by antique armoires, many of which have been in Crown warehouses, waiting to be restored to their places. In a recent generous donation courtesy of Albert D. Cohen, Chairman and Chief

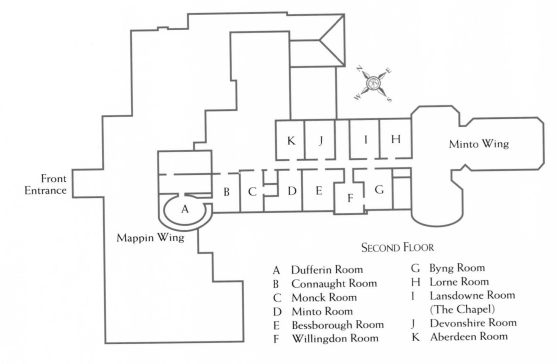

Front Entrance

Minto Wing

Mappin Wing

SECOND FLOOR

A   Dufferin Room
B   Connaught Room
C   Monck Room
D   Minto Room
E   Bessborough Room
F   Willingdon Room

G   Byng Room
H   Lorne Room
I   Lansdowne Room
    (The Chapel)
J   Devonshire Room
K   Aberdeen Room

Vistas from the south side are magnificent. In winter, when the leaves have fallen, the Parliament Buildings can be seen.

Originally used by the governors general, their families and members of the household, the bedrooms today provide accommodation for official visitors and their entourages.

All of the guest rooms have private baths and original fireplaces, the painted-marble mantelpieces of which are in the process of restoration to their original finish.

Executive Officer, Sony of Canada Limited has contributed televisions of the latest design and technology for each suite.

All the rooms are named for former British occupants. The sitting room named after Lord Byng and the attached bedroom commemorating Lord Willingdon make up one of the most attractive guest suites.

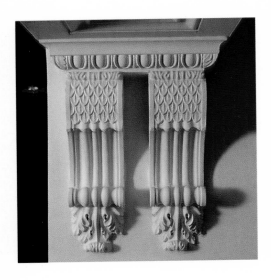

Typical turn-of-the-century architectural wall mounts adorn the space above the stairway (left).

One can see autographed photographs of Lord and Lady Byng, given by Friends of Rideau Hall, John and Joyce Pearkes. There is an historical connection here – Mr. Pearkes is the son of a former aide-de-camp to Lord Byng.

In the past few years, descendants of some of the previous governors general were approached in the hope that they would donate historical memorabilia. As a result, in 1988 a beautiful Regency mirror once used at Chatsworth, the Devonshires' seat in England, was given for the Devonshire Room.

A delicate turn-of-the-century Louis XVI-style writing table graces the Connaught Room (above right).
Several chairs in the room were decorated by Princess Patricia.
The back splats feature a trophy of musical instruments (above).

ROYAL SUITE

The Royal Suite is comprised of three rooms named after Lord Dufferin, the Duke of Connaught and Lord Monck.

as a schoolroom for the Aberdeen children and as a sitting room for Princess Patricia of Connaught.

The Dufferin Room has been a familiar haven to visiting dignitaries for many years. In early days, this room was used as a drawing room by Thomas MacKay, as an interim ballroom during the occupancy of Lord Dufferin while the new one was being constructed, as a bedroom of the Marquess of Lorne,

The ornate plaster ceiling with its frieze of acanthus leaves and centre medallion of Scottish thistles is one of the finest early ornamental ceilings to survive in Canada. Its oval shape and its classic styling are in harmony with the English Regency fireplace in white marble.

90

The furniture has been assembled to adapt the essentially Victorian elegance of this room to modern tastes. The principal bed of the suite is of mahogany and walnut, covered with sumptuous linens donated by Pratesi Linens Canada Inc. A recent major refurbishing in a subtle palette of buff and cream complements the natural wood finishes of the period furnishings.

Portraits of Lady Hariot, Countess of Dufferin (above) and Frederick Temple Blackwood, First Earl of Dufferin and Governor General of Canada from 1872 to 1878 (top).

The resulting quiet interior lends itself to private moments of reflection.

The delicate birch turn-of-the-century settee and two matching chairs were handpainted with florals by Princess Patricia of Connaught.

Among the paintings from the Official Residences Collection is a snow scene in Ottawa painted by Princess Patricia in 1916 and presented to Government House. Below it stands a Louis XVI-style writing desk which first showed up in an undated photograph of the Princess, seated beside it in one of the chairs she decorated. These pieces have been fortuitously reunited.

Two Italian cabinets, circa 1755-65, originally purchased by Count Alezzi of Florence, were given by Mrs. Gerald Hamilton of Toronto. The restfully nostalgic ambiance of the Connaught Room is enhanced by intricate lace cutwork which graces the linens (above). The bed was first used by Princess Alice, Countess of Athlone, circa 1940 (left and above).

The Blue Shawl, a portrait of Alice
Fowler painted in 1923 by the Canadian
artist Charles Walter Simpson is on loan
from the National Gallery of Canada.
A copy of a portrait of Lady Monck,
painted after John Singer Sargent at the
request of Mrs. Norah Michener, was
acquired by Public Works Canada in
September 1974.

*The Dufferin Room is the principal room of the Royal Suite.
The settee dates from the time when Princess Patricia used the
brightly lit area as a studio (left).*
The Blue Shawl by Charles Walter Simpson (above).

The Connaught Room is an intimate sitting room, centrally located and accessible to the two bedrooms. Guests can relax or be briefed on the rest of the visit, read the daily newspapers or recapture the day's events on television. Breakfast is served here and on occasion, a light lunch.

The third room, the Monck Room, serves as an additional bedroom. Its handsome mahogany sleigh bed, or "French day bed" as it was called in its time, is a North American adaptation of

the Empire style and was manufactured in Picton, Ontario, in the mid-19th century. It sustains the atmosphere of pleasant reverie 🎋

The Monck Room features a period sleigh bed dressed with Pratesi linens (above).
The room is dominated by a classical mahogany-finished armoire, now used as an entertainment centre (right).

CHAPEL

Lady Aberdeen's notes on her initial reaction to Rideau Hall included:

We think we shall be very comfy here and we are already making arrangements for building a little chapel on our own account where an old conservatory now stands at the end of the house.[3]

The "dear new little wooden chapel" which was ready by Christmas Eve of 1893, was situated at the far end of the house, in a space now occupied by administrative offices. It was the epitome of simplicity with its plain pine walls and roof, red matting on the floor, coloured glass in the windows, and straight-backed chairs.

Near the end of the Aberdeen era there was a farewell dinner at Rideau Hall. At the chapel service which followed, rousing choruses of "God be with you till we meet again" were sung, and many tears were shed. Lord Aberdeen presented the chapel to the government; it was ultimately dismantled and reconstructed in a mission district.

The Duchess of Connaught turned her attention to the Anglican parish church, St. Bartholomew's[4]. She installed, among other things, the small organ which had been in storage since the removal of the Aberdeens' chapel from the grounds.

 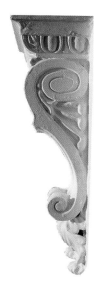

MAPPIN WING

In the front of the house, overlooking the fountain, is an area called "The Mappin," a few steps up from the second-floor corridor. The name apparently stems from the discovery by an aide-de-camp of a stuffed grizzly bear which reminded him of Mappin Terrace, the polar bear enclosure at Regent's Park, London.

During state visits, some rooms of The Mappin may be pressed into service to house the accompanying party. The utilitarian space comprises adequate bedrooms, sitting rooms and a hospitality suite.

Three aides-de-camp, representing the different branches of the Canadian armed services, live in a six-room apartment above this area

During the Vanier mandate, a new chapel, the first since the Aberdeens' time, was set up for daily mass in a former bedroom. On Sundays, the Vaniers attended churches of many denominations.

Many changes have taken place over the years. The Chapel became ecumenical, and following the wishes of the Micheners, was dedicated to both Anglican and Roman Catholic services by Bishop Reed and Canon Hermas Guindon, in the presence of Her Majesty the Queen, on July 2, 1967.

Now after all the challenges to alter the small room, it is an oasis of tranquillity. It has recently undergone a further metamorphosis. A new bird's-eye maple floor harmonizes with a turn-of-the-century maple and walnut armoire that has been restored to its original magnificent state and now serves as a repository for vestments and prayer books. The Chapel is graced by a superb silver cross and matching candlesticks, the gift of Théodore Arcand, Ottawa

3 Sept. 26, 1893, in R.H. Hubbard: Rideau Hall, p.77.

4 There have been other vice-regal associations with St. Bartholomew's: Lord Monck laid the cornerstone of the parish church in 1868; The Duke of Connaught donated a stained-glass window to commemorate members of Rideau Hall staff who lost their lives in World War I.

The Chapel, a tranquil retreat for guests and residents, was completed in the mid 1980s (above top). A decorative ceiling detail (above).

BEHIND

THE

SCENES

Beyond the red-carpeted corridors, the salons and the state apartments, there are tiled floors and a spartan, efficient air. This is where one really appreciates the word "rambling" as applied to a house. Apart from kitchens, storerooms, linen rooms, laundries and a wine cellar, there are any number of small offices, two meeting rooms and a library, all supporting the daily activities at Rideau Hall. A newcomer may need a map and compass; one can easily get lost.

Everyone who passes the red-coated ceremonial footguards and enters the front door receives hospitality that is formal to some degree. The care and judgement of such matters is within the purview of the hospitality staff, who play a pivotal role in the life of Rideau Hall. In 1934, a manual of protocol known as the Green Book was written by Alan Lascelles, the secretary to Lord Bessborough. Now, 60 years later, a former ambassador and chief of protocol is editing a modern version, taking care to maintain tradition.

A housekeeper attends to one of the countless details — a daily ritual (right).
The Maître d'Hôtel and footmen are prepared for a reception (opposite).

It is most important that arriving visitors, who may be apprehensive, be put immediately at ease. This may be accomplished simply by a smile and a greeting from the cloakroom attendant in either of Canada's official languages.

The hospitality department is made up of housekeepers, the Maître d'Hôtel and his staff, and the Chef, Sous-chef and the cooks.

The present Maître d'Hôtel, who lives on the grounds, has more than 25 years of experience at Rideau Hall. Within his domain are footmen, pantry-men and housekeepers. The footmen have been trained to "work with their eyes," in silence, to observe and attend smoothly to the needs and wishes of all visitors. The staff may be called upon to ensure that there is a crackling fire, an elegant table setting, an exquisite meal, or a car waiting at the door.

Folding linen napkins has been honed to a fine art (above). The Maître d'Hôtel ensures that the selection of wine is suitable for that night's banquet (right).

In matters of the condition and functioning of the household, the Maître. d'Hôtel is satisfied with nothing less than perfection. Housekeeping tasks are performed discreetly with constant vigilance. There are inventories to be checked and maintained.

Footmen regularly check the china to ensure that no damaged pieces are used (above).
Periodically, the entire collection of silver is buffed by machine to maintain its sheen (right).

All silver must be handled with white gloves, and lovingly polished only by experienced hands using gentle methods which are a house secret.

Meals are served in many locations throughout the house. Upon arising, guests may expect to be greeted in the Breakfast Room, although on a bright morning the Verandah is also a favourite spot. Luncheons are generally served in one of the dining rooms, but again, as a pleasant diversion, a midday meal may be offered in the Greenhouse, in a milieu of brightness and fragrance. This space is a wondrous room when the windows are enveloped in snow.

For grand state dinners, the Ballroom is furnished with tables. Equally large buffets may be presented in the Tent Room, under the thoughtful gaze of past governors general. If a particular space is not exactly right, it is adapted by using screens, furnishings and plants.

Candles and flowers are selected with the guest of honour in mind. The floral designers often use the colours in the flag of the country of the state visitor. Each meal is served with exquisite attention to detail.

100

An elaborate display of flowers, arranged by greenhouse staff, adds a splash of colour and natural beauty to the Dining Room table (right).
The pastry chef offers a selection of delicacies that taste every bit as good as they look (opposite).

The Chef and his staff form a versatile team. Each has a particular talent, contributing to a fusion cuisine. Essentially French, it incorporates the Italian tradition of purity of ingredients, the elegant simplicity of Japanese and Chinese menus, the tangy elements of Thai food and the sensuous spices of India. The ingredients in this unique cuisine are for the most part Canadian; vegetables such as carrots, peas, beans, tomatoes, cucumbers, squash and herbs are grown in the Rideau Hall garden. The herbs are frozen for use in winter. Menus are planned so that foods typically Canadian can be used – New Brunswick fiddleheads, tender Ontario lamb, western beef, fine lobster and scallops from both coasts. Maple syrup produced on the grounds often finds its way into the desserts. A cool cellar provides a variety of imported as well as Canadian wines.

*The Chef and his assistants prepare for a large banquet
(above and opposite).
Herbs are picked fresh from the Rideau Hall garden (above top).*

Last-minute refinements to the presentation of the food are made in serveries adjacent to the various rooms. Recent renovations in the hospitality department have improved efficiency and working conditions.

Dinner places are set meticulously. Tablecloths are given a last-minute ironing on the table to be sure they are creaseless. Chairs are placed with mathematical precision. Plates, glasses and silver are aligned.

The Chef presides over the modern kitchen with its gleaming commercial equipment and commodious working surfaces. Here, 70,000 meals are prepared annually – from a luncheon for two to a state dinner for 100, or a garden party for 15,000. The kitchen is open every day of the year.

A work of culinary artistry prepared by the Pastry Chef (left).
Pristine, perfectly smooth tablecloths are essential (above).
A commissionaire on night patrol (right).

A basement cafeteria is available
to staff members for lunch. Also "below
stairs" is a small but highly efficient
laundry with the latest equipment.

*The Tent Room chandelier undergoes routine maintenance
prior to a reception (opposite).*
*Mail is delivered throughout Rideau Hall several times
daily (above).*

Rolling out the red carpet for the arrival of visiting heads of state is a time-honoured ritual (opposite).
A master cabinetmaker oversees the ongoing maintenance of the collection (left).
The in-house carpentry shop is equipped to handle all repairs and woodworking (above).

111

Unlike the kitchens and house-keeping section, the offices are deserted in the evenings and on weekends. Years ago, unmarried staff members lived on the premises. The men lived in what is now the office space and the women lived in the back portion of the private quarters. Other than the residents, the only persons who live in the building are the three aides-de-camp.

The present Valet has been on the staff of Rideau Hall for over 30 years. Both he and the Maître d'Hôtel have had the opportunity to observe the activities of another famous house, Buckingham Palace.

Aides-de-camp tend to the many details during the Governor General's official visits. Behind them is a portrait of the Earl of Aberdeen (seventh Governor General of Canada) (opposite). The Valet prepares one of the Governor General's uniforms (above).

The Valet must be aware of the details of the Governor General's forthcoming agenda and ensure that the appropriate attire is taken from the wardrobe, pressed and hung out in readiness.

suggestions that one or the other become a patron of a worthy cause, enquiries about the role of the Governor General and a host of other matters, the office staff answer hundreds of telephone calls

The Valet travels with the Governor General on all his official excursions.

Other activities behind the scenes are almost too numerous to mention. They range from ensuring that the Governor General's standard flies when he or she is in residence, to handling the baggage associated with all the comings and goings. With endless requests for Their Excellencies' attendance at functions,

daily. They mail out countless invitations and open, sort and answer many letters in the same period. Adding to the general air of unrelenting bustle are the gifts to be wrapped for presentation and rooms to be prepared for state visits.

Volunteers wrap official gifts in Rideau Hall's personalized paper and ribbons for a state visit to Asia (above).
Household staff meet regularly to coordinate the many invitations extended to the Governor General and spouse, and plan the schedule (right).

There is security on the grounds at all times. In short, the devoted staff generally ensure that the welcome and hospitality extended at Rideau Hall are second to none. Every departing guest should carry away happy impressions

The Governor General's personal secretary sets the daily agenda on the desk (above).
The three official chauffeurs must keep their limousines in impeccable condition (above and right).
On special occasions, an assortment of home-made delicacies including jams, chutneys and maple syrup are offered as gifts to guests as a memento of their visit (overleaf).

House Speciality
Spécialité de la maison

"Rideau... is a long, two-storied villa, with a small garden on one side of it and a hedge which bounds our property on the other — so that at this time of year there is really no place to walk."

[Lady Dufferin, Journal, November 2, 1872.]

In contrast, visitors in the 1990s may stroll through the grounds alone, or join a guided walking tour through beautiful lawns, along the avenue serving royalty and heads of state. You will see trees planted by visiting dignitaries and hear intriguing tales of the residence and its inhabitants.

III

GREENHOUSES,

GARDENS AND

GROUNDS

$\mathcal{S}$tepping from the house onto the bricked pathway of the long greenhouse is like walking into a perfumed mist. The aroma of gardenias, lemons, lilies, sweet night-scented stocks and a host of flowers that were in your grandmother's garden is every bit as exquisite as the visual delight before you. Juniper topiaries, some looking as though they walked off a Persian carpet, others with fanciful spirals, compete for attention with the exotic jungle of the Palm House beyond.

Two young Canadians present daffodils to His Excellency, launching the Canadian Cancer Society Campaign (above). Beautiful spring flowers give a foretaste of the outdoor splendours to come (centre).

It is here, in these greenhouses, that the National Capital Commission's horticulturalist and his team nurture plants and flowers for other official residences in the National Capital Region.

About 1,100 square metres are under glass. Controlled environments range from tropical to boreal, providing ideal conditions for the propagation, recuperation and flourishing of a wide

range of plants. All plant material, once rooted, is kept in pots placed on beds of gravel. One potted Ponderosa lemon tree bears fruit weighing more than 500 grams each. The Chef uses them for tea, makes lemon sorbets, sauces, and pots of lemon curd. Some of the potted jade trees, among which are gifts of the world-renowned Canadian photographer Yousuf Karsh, have been at Rideau Hall for at least 50 years.

Stunning orchids that were presented to Her Excellency during an AIDS event in Montreal (above).

Another tree, a Buddhist pine, was donated by the Government of The United States of America to thank Canadians for helping six of their embassy staff escape from Tehran in January 1980, during the Iranian hostage crisis.

In the floral design area, cut flowers are kept in a refrigerated room until needed. Nothing is wasted; cut flowers are arranged, recycled and dried.

The Palm House is a favourite stop on public tours of the grounds of Rideau Hall. Here growth is so vigorous that many of the larger trees have to be pruned frequently. A cashew banana tree produces small, sweet bananas. The massed foliage around a pond and small waterfall creates a lush and exotic air. The goldfish have multiplied, obviously finding conditions optimal – perhaps because

virtually no pesticides are used, and when they are, only those of the lowest toxicity. Instead, to control plant diseases, the gardeners rely on biological insect control. Visitors are asked not to throw coins into the pond because the metal is not good for the fish, but some can't resist the temptation 🦎

Plants of all kinds flourish under the watchful eye of the greenhouse technician.

OUTSIDE

The vice-regal residence and adjoining greenhouses are set within a park-like environment which in Thomas MacKay's day was much more extensive.

When MacKay built Rideau Hall, he sited it in the middle of the 450-hectare tract he had purchased. This included much of what is now the Ottawa neighbourhood of New Edinburgh and the Village of Rockcliffe Park. Even while the government was renting the estate, before it had purchased Rideau Hall in 1868, Lord Monck began changing the landscape.

A bird's-eye view of the estate in early autumn (above top). The historic garage building, circa 1860, was originally used as a stable (above).

During Lord Monck's residency, the basic shape of the estate was created. A new avenue of approach was built and the farm sector enhanced, conservatory and greenhouse built, and ornamental gardens planted. Rideau Cottage, an English-style turn-of-the-century country home, was built to house the Governor General during the summers. It is now used as home for the Secretary to the Governor General.

Fencing was installed on the perimeter and within the grounds, paths were made throughout the estate, and trees lavishly planted. A permanent cricket pavilion erected in 1875 is still used by local clubs.

Landscape changes may have been made piecemeal, but they were unified, after a fashion, by the prevailing ideals of the English country estate. At one time, a herd of cows was kept, and hay used to be cut regularly. There was an orchard and a vegetable garden, much larger than the present one where fresh herbs are cut daily. Trees were grown and cut down with regularity. New roads and paths were laid and then changed again.

A second wave of significant change was effected in the early 1900s. From this point on, the major alterations and enhancements of the landscape

The perennial task of maintaining the grounds (above).
The sights and sounds on the cricket pitch are reminiscent
of a bygone era (right).

occurred mainly in the ornamental gardens although architectural and structural changes were also made. Lady Minto and Lady Grey were avid gardeners who enlarged the scope of flower gardening on the upper lawns.

The practice of planting thousands of tulip bulbs on the entrance grounds began with these two chatelaines.

Thousands of tulip bulbs planted each year erupt in an explosion of springtime colour (above top).
Both residents and staff use the Rideau Hall tennis courts (above).

During the term of Lord Byng and his enthusiastic gardener wife, and also during the time of the Willingdons, the layout of the present gardens was consolidated. At this time, the spacious Verandah was built beside the Long Gallery, and tennis courts were installed. Lady Byng, who as a little girl had lived at Rideau Hall when her father was on Lord Monck's staff, planted clumps of maple

trees and beds of roses and irises and had a rock garden laid out with a pond and a corner for wild trilliums and orchids.

Princess Juliana, later Queen Juliana of the Netherlands, and her children lived in Rideau Hall during part of 1940 as guests of the Earl of Athlone and Princess Alice. Later, the Princess rented a home for herself in Rockcliffe Park. The tulips of Rideau Hall and the National Capital Region are a continuing gift from the Netherlands, instituted by Queen Juliana in gratitude for the hospitality shown to herself and her mother,

Queen Wilhelmina, throughout World War II.

Sugaring-off is another popular activity, first documented in 1911, that continues to this day.

❖

The northwestern corner of the property has been left wooded since the time of Thomas MacKay.

This area became popular for winter pastimes such as skating, curling and tobogganing. Next to the woodland rink, a small log cabin was built to be used as a warm-up hut for skaters.

The original perimeter fence, circa 1900, forms a fitting backdrop to the majestic gardens (opposite).
The skating rink is open to the public. (above left).
Maple trees are tapped early each spring. The maple syrup is used in Rideau Hall both in the kitchen and as gifts to guests (above top).
Tobogganing parties are held for families from the various embassies (above).

A brick laundry built in 1876 was later converted into two cottages and rented to married servants. A year later, a round, brick gasometer building was erected to supply a reliable source of power to the estate.

In 1895, a one-storey wooden dairy building was constructed on the edge of the bush next to the back access road. It was later moved. A variety of smaller service buildings came and went over the years.

An historic house commonly referred to as 11 Rideau Gate at the Thomas Street entrance is used as an information centre by Rideau Hall tour guides.

A magnificent maple tree in autumn foliage borders the tennis courts.

Other interesting features are scattered throughout the grounds, including a cemetery for pets, various commemorative stones, and a weathering steel and bronze sculpture given by the George and Helen Vari Foundation. A totem pole, a gift to Viscount Alexander from the Kwakiutl carver Mungo Martin, was relocated in the Lady Byng Rock Garden during the Michener years.

From its earliest vice-regal days, the residents and federal caretakers of the estate have been fully conscious that the site is constantly in the public eye, the grounds having a role to play in the ceremonial life of Canada. Visiting dignitaries have left tangible evidence of their stay by planting trees that bear plaques with their names.

The grounds come to life in the spring. School patrollers whose brave actions have saved lives are awarded medals. The full Ceremonial Guard meets the Governor General, their Honorary Colonel, for annual inspection prior to taking up their summer duties. This colourful ceremony provides an opportunity for Government House to show its appreciation to the sentries who stand guard throughout the summer.

The distinctive octagonal guardhouse stands on the perimeter of the grounds by the front gate (above left).
The original gasometer building is used by administrative staff these days (top).
One of the many trees planted by distinguished visitors (above).

The annual summer garden party has always been a feature of the Rideau Hall social calendar. In the Lorne era, an autumn garden party was also held. When the Aberdeens were at Rideau Hall, tennis and croquet were played during such events. A feature of the parties, which continues to the present day, was the music of the scarlet-coated Governor General's Foot Guards Band. Until 1976, these were formal, invitation-only affairs with guests drawn from the Canadian

Order of Precedence: the diplomatic corps, Privy Council members, judges, senators, members of Parliament and deputy ministers. In addition, anyone who had signed the visitors' book at Rideau Hall in the year prior to the garden party received an invitation. In these years, approximately 4,000 attended.

The totem pole, a gift during the mandate of Viscount Alexander (17th Governor General of Canada), stands in the Lady Byng Rock Garden (left).
The pet cemetery (above).
A romantic pool lies at the heart of the Lady Byng Rock Garden (right).

Early in the Léger mandate, it was decided to advertise the garden party and invite the general public. Today, a large annual garden party is held in June where as many as 15,000 Canadians meet Their Excellencies in the informal setting of the grounds.

The garden party reinforces the Governor General's direct link with people from across the country. Since 1991, the Canadian Broadcasting Corporation has hosted an outdoor concert as part of the festivities. This musical event is broadcast nationally on Canada Day.

In summer, outdoor concerts are held every Sunday afternoon. Families are encouraged to attend. On such afternoons, cheers from the white-clad cricketers can be heard across the grounds.

On Hallowe'en, the driveway is enlivened with witches, ghosts and goblins as children living in the area converge upon Rideau Hall. The aides-de-camp and footmen dress up in costume and lie in wait among the trees or near the fountain. Once inside the foyer, children and young adults receive their treats.

Hundreds of children come to Rideau Hall on Hallowe'en and receive vice-regal treats.
An impressive backyard view of Rideau Hall and its grounds (opposite).

In winter, staff and the public enjoy weekend skating on the rink. On weekday afternoons, teachers may be seen entering the grounds with children, skates over their shoulders.

Over the years, despite all the changes going on within the house, the grounds have retained a feeling of timelessness and serenity. Wild animals such as beavers, foxes, rabbits, ground-hogs and squirrels find the grounds as much of a haven as do humans.

The Rideau Hall grounds are significant in Ottawa's horticultural history, forming a unique country estate in the middle of the city. Here is one of only two surviving 19th-century land-scapes in the capital. The other is the nearby Beechwood Cemetery, where some of the former Government House staff are interred 🦫

The changing of the Ceremonial Guard is particularly colourful during the autumn (above).
The George and Helen Vari Foundation donated the steel garden sculpture, Osmosis, by Susan Stromberg-Stein (opposite).

The day on which she arrived at Rideau Hall, Lady Dufferin, wife of the third Governor General of Canada, wrote that "the inevitable bare tables and ornamentless rooms have a depressing effect." If only she could see it now.

In those areas that have been refurbished and rearranged, it is, in a word, even by the most sophisticated standards, breathtaking. Not only does one's heart swell with pride that this is Canada's metaphorical home, and belongs to all of us, but we can also be fairly certain that a no more inviting atmosphere exists in any other official residence, anywhere in the world.

IV

BUILDING

THE

COLLECTION

A pair of Coalport yellow ground-shell-decorated vases,
circa 1810, part of a large collection given by
Joan Henderson and the late Gordon Henderson (above).
An untitled painting by Québec artist Réne Richard is part
of the Official Residences Collection (above right).
This Riopelle painting was the bequest of the estate
of Dr. R.H. Hubbard (opposite).

It is apparent to anyone walking through Rideau Hall that skilled and loving hands have refurbished the public and state rooms. Throughout this book, mention has been made of many generous gifts that have allowed the present residents and the designer, collaborating closely, to leave an enriched legacy for future generations of Canadians. The Canadiana Fund and Friends of Rideau Hall have largely made this possible. Both groups have encouraged Canadians to participate in the ongoing restoration of this residence.

This book can give you a glimpse of what has been achieved in the past. In the future, other residents will undoubtedly further enhance the state rooms. Many people have responded positively upon learning that Rideau Hall could be improved by the acquisition of beautiful artifacts. Although past residents have made important contributions to the Collection, the first major Canadian donors were Bernard and Sylvia Ostry.

It is apparent that many Canadians want to express love of country through their giving.

Although the restoration has been a personal project of Her Excellency, Mrs. Gerda Hnatyshyn, it would not have been possible without the support, cooperation and encouragement of the Official Residences Council and the National Capital Commission. Both were essential to its success.

Dreaming of the Far North, by Ted Harrison, C.M., is a gift from the artist.
A unique crooked-neck carved goose, by an unknown artist circa 1940, was a gift from Jean-Marie Roy (above).

The big country house of 1838 has been brought into the last decade of the 20th century. Its interiors have been reawakened, and now it stands as a national symbol, proud to welcome all Canadians

The late 18th-century Louis XV pine armoire was a gift acquired through the Canadiana Fund (above left).
A cup-like shell flanked by leaves is centred on the upper stile of the armoire (above).

Cap avant Gros-Morne, *by Claude Picher, was donated by the artist.*

139

Caramaba, by Benoît Côté, a gift from the artist (top).
Mother and Child, *a soapstone sculpture by Moses*
Aupuluktuk, was a gift to Mrs. Norah Michener, who gave
it to Rideau Hall (above).

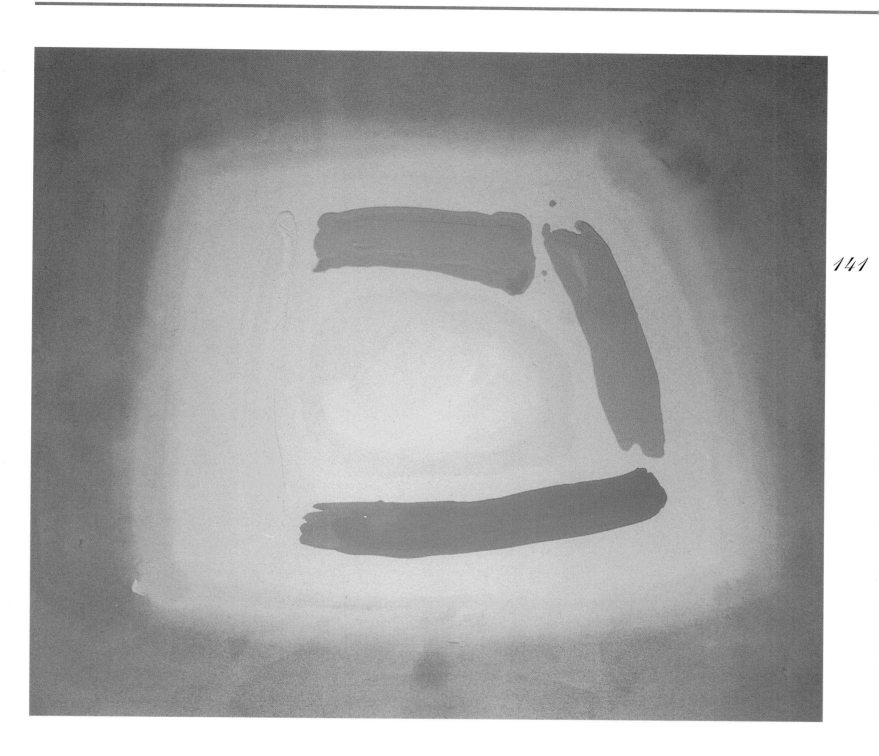

Pacific Gateway (164), *by John Koerner, a gift from*
the artist (left).
This painting entitled AC-87-59, by William Perehudoff, was
given to Rideau Hall by the artist (above).

*The Sèvres-style urns with gilt mounts were a gift from
Mr. Stuart Clyne and Mrs. Valentine D. Gamage (right).
A Regency mirror plays up the drama of the marble Victorian
mantel in the Devonshire Room (above).*

143

The portrait of Lord Tweedsmuir by Jongers was a gift
from John William Buchan (above).
The Royal Crown Derby urn commemorating Canada's
centennial in 1967 is part of a set that was made and contributed
by Henry Birks and Sons Ltd. (above right).
A rare sterling silver punch-bowl from the Henry Birks Collection,
circa 1900, was donated by Mr. and Mrs. Vincent Paul (right).

Artist Donald C. Phalen donated this life-size loon
which placed first in the 1992 World Decoy Carving
Championship (above right).
Chinese gourd-shaped vases featuring the mark of the
Reign of Ch'ien Lung (1736-1795) were a gift from
Keith Johnson (above).
An English porcelain tea-bowl and plate, believed to have been
made for Lord Amherst on the occasion of an 1823 journey to
India, donated by Mrs. Joan Redfern (right).

145

One of a pair of late 19th-century Sèvres urns on gilded plinths
that were a gift from Mrs. Dorothy Alexander and Mrs.
Benjamin Luxenberg in memory of Mr. and Mrs. A.J. Freiman.

REFERENCES

Much of the historical information presented in this book is derived from materials held in the archives of Rideau Hall. Other sources are listed below.

Conlogue, Ray. "Musical icons honoured at awards." *The Globe and Mail*, November 29, 1993.

Fardin, Linda Dicaire, Edwinna von Baeyer, and Mark Laird. *Rideau Hall Landscape Conservation Study*. Ottawa: National Capital Commission, 1991.

Hault, Esther. *Rideau Hall: An historical interiors research report*. Ottawa: National Capital Commission, 1989.

Hubbard, R.H. *Rideau Hall: An illustrated history of Government House*. Montreal: McGill-Queen's University Press, 1977.

Rohr, Joan Michener, with Terence Heath. *Memories of a Governor General's Daughter*. Toronto: Bedford House, 1990.

148

GOVERNORS

GENERAL OF

CANADA

The Viscount Monck, 1867 - 1868

The Baron Lisgar of Lisgar and Bailieborough, 1869 - 1872

The Earl of Dufferin, 1872 - 1878

The Marquess of Lorne, 1878 - 1883

The Marquess of Lansdowne, 1883 - 1888

The Baron Stanley of Preston, 1888 - 1893

The Earl of Aberdeen, 1893 - 1898

The Earl of Minto, 1898 - 1904

The Earl Grey, 1904 - 1911

Field Marshal His Royal Highness The Duke of
     Connaught and Strathearn, 1911 - 1916

The Duke of Devonshire, 1916 - 1921

General The Baron Byng of Vimy, 1921 - 1926

The Viscount Willingdon of Ratton, 1926 - 1931

The Earl of Bessborough, 1931 - 1935

The Baron Tweedsmuir of Elsfield, 1935 - 1940

Major General The Earl of Athlone, 1940 - 1946

Field Marshal The Viscount Alexander of Tunis, 1946 - 1952

The Right Honourable Vincent Massey, 1952 - 1959

Major General The Right Honourable Georges P. Vanier, 1959 - 1967

The Right Honourable Daniel Roland Michener, 1967 - 1974

The Right Honourable Jules Léger, 1974 - 1979

The Right Honourable Edward Richard Schreyer, 1979 - 1984

The Right Honourable Jeanne Sauvé, 1984 - 1990

The Right Honourable Ramon John Hnatyshyn, 1990 - 1995